Chalkmarks on Stone

CHALKMARKS ON STONE

Carol Moldaw

La Alameda Press • Albuquerque

Grateful acknowledgment is made to the National Endowment for the Arts, which provided a fellowship during which many of these poems were written, and also to the Virginia Center for the Creative Arts and The MacDowell Colony.

Some of the poems in this collection have appeared in the following publications and anthologies:

Another Desert: Jewish Poets of New Mexico (Sherman Asher): "Lines Begun on Yom Kippur"; *First Intensity*: twenty-four hexagrams from "Another Part of the Field"; *Frank* (Paris): "The Jewish Cemetery at Penang"; *Hanging Loose*: two hexagrams from "Another Part of the Field"; *Manoa*: "At the Marketstall," "Seed Bolls," "Winged Victory"; **New Mexico Poetry Renaissance: A Community on Paper** (Red Crane):"Beads of Rain," "Our New Life," "Summer Sublet"; *The New Republic*: "Bosque del Apache," "Chalkmarks on Stone"; *The New Yorker*: "Beads of Rain"; *The Onset Review*: "The Trout"; *Orion*: "The Butterfly"; *Partisan Review*: "After a Long Journey"; **The Practice of Peace** (Sherman Asher): eighteen hexagrams from "Another Part of the Field"; *Puerto del Sol*: twenty-four hexagrams from "Another Part of the Field"; *River Styx*: "Drumming for the Matryoshka," "Summer Sublet"; *Solo*: twelve hexagrams from "Another Part of the Field"; *Southwest Review*: "Initials"; *THE*: "Beads of Rain"; *The Threepenny Review*: "Relict"; *Triquarterly*: "The Peony".

La Alameda Press
9636 Guadalupe Trail NW
Albuquerque, New Mexico 87114

for my parents
Stuart and Phyllis Moldaw

CONTENTS

I
Chalkmarks on Stone

II
At the Market Stall

III
Another Part of the Field

I
Chalkmarks on Stone

Beads of Rain

Each day I've looked
into the beveled mirror
on this desk, vainly
asking it questions
reflection cannot answer.

Outside, fog and frost
and silver olive leaves.
I can see at most
a half field's depth,
then the trees are lost
in the gauzy mist
like thin unbraceleted arms
swallowed by billowing sleeves.

I'd like to face
that stringent looking glass
transparent to myself
as beads of rain
pooled on a green leaf.

But ever self-composed
in self-regard,
and my eyes opaque
as a dancer's leotard,
to see straight through myself
I need what love supplies:
its dark arrows, dear,
not its white lies.

Relict

The tree itself,
being forbidden,
creates disequilibrium:

in Eden,
as at home,
I'm sure the fruit
looked very sweet
while still on the branch,

like the smell
of fresh unlit tobacco,
like a man not yet kissed.

Relict, he said.
Vestigial.
The heart of the old forest,
the only patch
of these feelings I have left.

Unused to the timbre
of his voice,
across the restaurant table

I stroked his arm,
the new word so delicious,
and the bone of his wrist.

While in Eden,
there was no end
to Eden, you could walk
for years and never cross
a border, never trespass.

But now, there is
no garden, only this fruit
still left to eat.

Chalkmarks on Stone

1.

I let the thermometer slide into place,
and think of Persephone waiting for Dis
to tuck another seed under her tongue.
Her mother's daughter, her own mistress,
from the first implacable thrust she was his.
She tallies their days with chalkmarks on stone.
Circles ring those days they make love.
Anticipation's a form of bliss,
her face tilting up like a baby bird's.
Red seed, red juice, raw mouths, red kiss:
a new row, the first marks tinged with blood.
She sees that time comes down to this—
endless cycles scratched in stone
that chronicle her barrenness.

2.

The best of Hades' healers and
the worst line up to treat the Queen
of the Dead behind her lacquered screen.
Some take her pulse; some hold her hand.
One reads the iris of her eye
and gives her drops to feed her blood.
One recommends she bathe in mud.
One flushes out her womb with dye.
Daydreaming over her birth chart,
she looks for clues to "if" and "when."
She breathes in hope like oxygen,
then holds her breath so the tears won't start.

3.

Not for all the jewels in her tears,
the sapphires, flawless diamonds, pearls
she so unstintingly pours forth,
would he, by any sign, imperil
his standing as a god, his self-worth,
and let her know how these last years
unmanned him, made him greedy as a child
who's fed, but grabs at any teat,
wailing for his mother's milk.
He keeps Hades' coffers stockpiled,
but it's not for Dis to count their gold.
Her long hair's gold, soft as corn silk.
She sleeps while he untangles it.
Such things can't be bought or sold.
Such things are easily defiled.
He chokes, fighting down self-wrath.
She wakes to an avalanche of tears,
his tears, the minerals for their bath.

4.

Grass, pine, the dangling willow shoots,
elm and aspen leaves in bud,
her mother's softest rumpled sheets,
her chaste luxurious unmade bed,
the scattered sprouts of crocus—all
the earth done up in gorgeous green,
curtained and carpeted for her arrival,
months before fields turn to grain,
with time to bask in the strong light
of her mother's solar-paneled house,
eating her fruits, happy to let
the sun burn off last winter's haze.

5.

She knows the dead, knows how they toil
in furnaces, quarries, mines that yield
a flinty harvest beneath the subsoil.
She's seen them let salt run through their hands,
the way they once had sifted through grain.
But where are the unborn concealed?
Night after restless night, search beams
blaze a dead-end trail through lands
whose border-guards patrol her dreams.
Though once, awake, she thought she saw—
unsteady as two newborn fawns—
her children standing in the rain,
waiting for her to come and draw
them in. She reached, and they were gone.

6.

Mornings, in the garden, pulling weeds,
or walking by fields of purple loosestrife,
Persephone thinks back to when,
in love, not caring what would happen,
laughing, she opened her mouth to Dis
to taste his pomegranate seeds
for the first time. Both sweet and tart,
they readied her to be his wife.
She bends to gather fruit that's fallen
ripened in her mother's lap.
Grapes are browning on the trellis.
She'll be home before the cold snap.
Each year her mother says she won't part
with her; each year she lets her go.
Dressed in Autumn's cooling mist,
she carries home a handful of pollen
she culled last spring from the wild meadow
where he first caught her by the wrist.

Summer Sublet

Sunlight sharp enough to slice
black-eyed Susans from their stems,
to sliver stone, so that a wall,
unmortared, laid with river rock
and slab, shimmers in the heat.

But once inside, the flagstone chills
like a gin and tonic, like when
you chew the cubes, and I shiver.
At noon, it's too dark to read a book
without a lamp, too dark to tell

the scalloped tin *retablo* of Mary
that leans on the corner fireplace mantel
from Grandma's hand-colored tintypes
taken and saved from the shtetl.
I lie on my side on the bed and read,

or else I sit at the all-purpose table,
make phone calls, and look out the window.
"One day at a time," my neighbor's car,
parked on the narrow washboard road,
reminds me. "One day at a time."

I watch him string a *ristra*, red
electric chiles, from his door.
In Asia, he also strung lights, something
electronic, a civilian during war.
He showed me a room in his landlord's house,

a room without floor or ceiling,
the windows strafed with bullet holes
where someone tried to collect on a debt.
The room was in back where the house had sunk.
Testing a warped board with my toe,

I placed my hot plate, desk, and shelves
before coming to, and saying *no*.
New York's as far as Kiev, except
I call, except, like Katmandu,
this is a place the world treks through.

Our sublet's a house of ghosts, mostly
not ours. Not mine, the bearded dead
boyfriend whose photo's enshrined on a shelf,
with matches, a candle for us to light;
not mine, the broken violin,

or yours, the tongue-depressor cross,
the shards of Anasazi pots,
the freezer full of bread and bones.
Our ghosts are less effusive, not
entirely at home, and restlessly circle

rooms that themselves circuit endlessly
around a central dead-storage space.
Soon, though, they'll come into their own.
Meanwhile, stacks of years-old postcards,
leaning against books we've never read,

with love from people we haven't met,
are collecting dust we'll never dust.

From the picture window's chipped pitcher,
sunset pours out drinks pungent and sweet,
a peach margarita, a daiquiri with lime.

We lie face up on the half-made bed
while summer makes the most of us.
July breaks on our windowsill.
We're awash in its salty marinade
till August sears us on the grill.

The Trout

Under the hymnal
drone of water
that would drown a shout,
I hear you say,
your voice a whisper,
"Come see the trout."
We are down at the kill.

Loose threads of foam
spin out and drift
in the shoal of calm
where you dip your hand,
widening a rift
in the light's frayed band
with your open palm.

Glistening, mottled,
mother-of-pearl,
it leaps your grasp,
slippery as thought.
A glide and a swirl:
it's under a ledge
where it can't be caught.

"Give it your pledge
you won't kill it,"
I say, and you swear
you intend no harm,
your voice foursquare

while your fingers flit
from your dangling arm.

Testing your word,
or trusting your voice,
or hearing in it
the soft command
that leaves no choice,
like me the trout's lured
to feed from your hand.

Our New Life

If the field is thick
with horse shit and the garden
unplanted, and the roof
needs repair; if after the next storm
sand from the acequia
overflows and suffocates the marsh,
killing the cattails where redwinged blackbirds nest,
if the neighbors' horses overgraze our field,
if I am lonely,
if a WIPP truck overturns
going back and forth from Los Alamos
to the shifting salt pits in Carlsbad,
if we go away for a week
and miss the crab apple's blossoming,
the sheep shearing,
if it turns out I am allergic to Russian olives,
to chamisa, to rabbit grass,
if they pave our dirt road,
if the cat returns to her original owner,
if the walls need remudding after every storm,
if the doctor finds a problem,
if the beer cans and corn chip bags and whiskey bottles
pile up on the road
faster than we can collect them for the dump,
if the doctor doesn't know what is wrong,
if Los Alamos gets the contract
to manufacture or stockpile or do anything whatever
with nuclear warheads,
if I cut my foot on a rusty washing machine part

while walking down by the river,
if I get lost in the Barrancas,
if my heart keeps shrinking,
if my heart explodes—
will I ever again think to look
for the new moon's thinnest crescent,
will we ever crane our necks together
as we used to, name the stars,
turn down the cool sheets,
go to bed not exhausted,
arms linked in one constellation
that turns all night in sync with the sky?

After a Long Journey

Now you've ridden both elephant and camel;
now you've worn the sackcloth of remorse,

carried the assassin's sap-sticky blade,
the suppliant's lamp of sesame oil, and now

you've planted the warrior's leaf-tipped spear
in front of my mud hut, reclaiming your stake

in my yes and my no. The gong rings out your hour,
hour and gong both forged in a bellows-fed flame;

your forehead's three forked veins, a trident
throbbing as you stoke the coral bed of coals.

Seed Bolls

Early in May, nimble-fingered and fierce,
the wind pries free the cottonwoods' cotton.
Once she blows the feathery seed-bolls off
her palm, they drift, angling softly down,
choking the air, like miniature parachutes,
and land on the run; collect, swirling, in corners,
bunched up big as volleyballs, but weightless.

They float like algae on the pail of water
left out for the dog; they whisk through open doors
too fast to keep them out. Brooming only
re-activates them, like music at a dance.
Wet down, they foam and flatten like suds drained
of water; stick to the ground, to soles of shoes,
where they don't peel off, like leaves, but must be scraped.

I raked them, inhaled them, picked them one by one
like gray hairs, out of my hair, but balked at first
when told to toss a match on the breathy puffs
of down. Combustible as gasoline,
they caught before the lit match hit the ground.
The flame flared all at once but didn't last,
leaving us bits of char and crackled seed.

Initials

Not carved into the living tree,
but set in concrete
where a dead branch in the crotch
of the trunk had been sawn off—
our initials, still paired and couched
in the flare-backed love seat
of a stick-drawn heart.

I see it every time
I drive in, coming home, next to
the absence of his truck.

I suppose that apple tree
will blossom this spring as always,
first with pink-tinged buds
and then, shiny green leaves.

I suppose by the time the apples
have fallen, I'll be crouched
on my knees, wielding my garden spade
like a palette knife
to spackle over the rough-hewn lines
until that heart and all it encloses
are imperceptible to hand and eye,
like an underpainting,
which keeps on existing, hidden
and contained by whatever is to come.

The Peony

A man cups his fingers as if to bring them
to his lips to blow me a goodbye kiss,
or, as if he were Italian, to underscore
his words. He is not Italian; he is not
speaking; and he does not bring his fingers
to his lips. Gravely, they descend upon a peony
held up by the rim of its fishbowl vase.
Because I would be his, he tells me a secret
it is mine to know, all the while spreading
the silky petals with his slowly opening hand
so that the peony is made to bloom to its fullest,
until it is an open globe, overbrimming the vase.
Only now do I think of those paper flowers
that blossomed when we floated them in water,
as girls. The words of the secret blurred
as soon as I woke, but his light hand
gravely forcing the peony, *that* remains.

Eclipse

1.

At the beginning
of the end, you rhyme
your wedding vows
with a broken vase.
Marriage
suddenly bloats up,
brackish, bleeds
into miscarriage,
and one vowel shifts,
creating rupture
where once was rapture—

2.

Once it seemed enough, surviving an August
eclipse, a night woken in the pitch black,
both of you paranoid and drenched in sweat.
It was his dream but your pillow the one
wet with tears, and your flushed voice the one
overhauled to scream her words his dream
could not contain. It was your head you pummeled,
your fist, and your own hair you pulled, yourself
the self vacated for his nightmare to possess
while like a vapor trail you were dissolving
across morning's electrified and emptied sky.

How many things like that—survived, but now,
it seems, not surmounted? The petri dish
of five kaleidoscopic splitting cells,
five mandala-like embryos,
and one that sank in the endometrial mass,
sucked like a tick, but did not grow. Survived,
but not surmounted. Years of days divided
into months marked off and counted only
as not counting. Survived, but not surmounted.

3.

Two heads tilted down,
each askew on its own
axis, and reflecting
on the other, exerting
equal pull: was it love
revolved around poetry,
or poetry circled love?

Two constellations.
A butterfly and a bull.
Trading typescripts
at the kitchen table,
we scanned our selves
while still in draft,
reduced what we could
to questions of craft,

entrusting the rest
to the muse. Was it love
strayed from poetry?
Or poetry diverged
from love? Star-strands
getting pulled apart
as the universe expands.

4.

Two Brahman priests, male and female elders,
swaying atop two tapering bamboo towers,
the dead boy between them, his squarish bamboo pyre

festooned with photos, school books, clothes, the body
laid out and prayed over, ready to be lit.

The village street is empty but for us,
our parade: ourselves objects more foreign
to children watching in doorways than the cloth-

capped gamelan, their elfin xylophone hammers,
their hand-forged, bamboo-poled, resounding gongs.

At each crossroads the procession halts while the boy—
a younger brother?—riding the pyre dismounts
and it is turned three times—once for each world,

and another chance to formulate goodbye.
The tinny music puts me in a trance.

One night the sea lulls you and you sleep at its hem,
a devotee curled at the feet of the mother.
Another night, the tide's hemp-corded net

catches you up, trawls you off the sea floor,
sleepless, fevered, crashing into waves

of restless longing. All of that is over
for the boy. We are glad for him, it is good
to have it over, hard though it is to accept.

As gas lines are linked up, people milling
outside the cemetery walls wander

our way and introduce themselves; one man
acts as our guide and host: steers us away
from the acrid smoke, nudges us nearer the flames.

5.

In the umbra
of earth's shadow,
the full moon
illumes nothing.
Premonitions
orbit the pillow,
are flicked away
heedlessly as houseflies,
leaving only a flurry
of question marks
that float down
into the cone
of a dreamer's ear,
like blown dandelion
in that field
near Concord,
seedpods rattling
the turkey grass.
Next time these sheets
are shaken out,
a packet of lavender
falls from the folds.

6.

One night the sea lulls you
and you sleep at her hem,
a devotee curled at the feet
of the mother; one night
you thrash in the tide's
hemp-corded net, trawled

over waves, helpless
with longing. One day
you wake unappeased,
listening for the sea's
inflection, but you hear
only unquiet breathing.

One day you watch
and chant as a body
burns, and it is not
a Balinese boy
killed on a motorcycle
but your friend's husband,

dead of colitis.
How often you have stood
in front of your own husband,
leaning against him,
but now, in the parking lot,
watching smoke rise

from the incinerator,
you are sure his arms
will not encircle you again,
though they are strong
as ever, tightening over
your breasts while you weep.

7.

Handblown vials of Italian inks.
Oca, rosa, verde, viola.

A cigar box of letters.
A dozen different addresses.

Three pair of gold hoops.
Innumerable hopes.

The uncut pages of unwritten books.
Reams of rhymes.

A twenty-year's hoard of browning roses clipped
and poured like chianti into a liter carafe—

spilled out and crushed, to scent this cenotaph.

II
At the Market Stall

At the Market Stall

Counting out syllables like pinches of spice,
I choked on their dust, left everything unsaid.

The new moon withered in her cup of darkness.

The peacock closed his iridescent eyes,
his green-fringed fan, and walked, stiff-legged, away.

Turquoise and gold gravel, like filings of
an ant hill, like rubble, lie heaped in a tall mound,
cast from a poem's excavated center.

The node of no: lodged in my throat, a leafless
varnished stump; inexorable seal and stopper.

Then winter's clear acoustics; the pale sun's
slow recuperation; and this, which is mine.

Lines Begun on Yom Kippur

for Yehudis Fishman

1.

I picture you in a phone booth
as you say your mid-day prayer,
the receiver a prop in your hand.

No one pays any attention
except God, who accepts all charges,
always pleased to be called.

Now, picture me in full lotus,
amid a mandala of crystals,
in front of a burning candle.

If, as you say, this—
our earth—is God's basement,
then that explains the clutter

of co-existence, the profusion
of road maps, the pamphlets
and mislabeled boxes, but why

is it some of us rummage madly
while others sort through one crate
with infinitesimal care?

2.

In that room, I followed Innana down
and hung by my toes from a thorn tree;

I lay on my back watching the stars
inside the dome of my mother's womb;

I pulled at the gold and silver threads
in her green sari until they snapped;

I followed the dissolving clouds of my breath
but soon they amassed and darkened;

I lay drenched and stunned in that downpour;
I was pelted by stones yanked from my own pocket;

I left myself to die.
I walked to the window.

In a building across the way,
some old men were praying at Shul.

They were wearing skullcaps and tallisim.
Each held a prayer book to his breast.

I watched through my curtain while they davened,
bobbing and swaying to greet the Sabbath Queen.

3.

You taught me that the word, in Hebrew,
generates and, by its emanations,
keeps the world in existence;
that each verse in the Book of Lamentations
begins with a different letter,
so that there is an end to suffering.

You said the high should reach down
to elevate the low; that before the Fall,
Adam and Eve had bodies of light,
and, had they waited for the Sabbath,
sanctified, they could have had their fruit.
You said that nothing's so holy and open

as the open rift in a broken heart;
that miracle is catastrophe's correlative.
You said sleep contains a 60th, "a touch,"
of death; Torah, a touch of Heaven;
Sabbath, Paradise; and dreams, prophecy.
As for poetry . . . that you've left up to me.

4.

To hear the long and short piercing blasts
of the shofar, I sneaked into a synagogue
a few blocks from my house one Rosh Hashanah.
The service was almost over, so I slipped past
the men in dark suits that guard both doors,
as if I'd just been out stretching my legs.
I was wearing a dress my mother would approve of,
and I found an empty seat right on the aisle.
I even thought of joining that congregation,
but to me, the rabbi in his tall furred hat,
his white embroidered fur-trimmed flowing robe,
looked more like some kind of priest than a rabbi.
Could I, over time, have made up the censer and smoke
that seems closer in spirit to the Holy Ghost
than to the ghastly fumes from the Holocaust?
The cantor's voice filled out the airy dome.
I heard the longed-for sweet and raspy blasts,
then took a walk to the river before going home.

At the river, I leaned over the wooden piling.
Anchor lines clanked against houseboats and piers.
Pulling some cracker crumbs out of my pocket,
I cupped them against the wind in the palm of my hand.
Like errands, my sins easily slip my mind,
but I compiled a list from odds and ends
guessed at or remembered; it was years ago now,
but how much do categories of sins change?
You might lie to yourself one year, your spouse another;
have greed for money, power, greed for fame;
be vain about looks, or just be generally vain …

Gossiping's like a cold that runs its course,
no matter how you try to avoid it. Like envy,
it's hard to shake, but that year, I remember,
I took envy by its anorexic waist
and threw it into the river and watched it drown,
though the crumbs themselves floated in a cluster,
unspiraling as the current sped them away.

Wolf

Prayer shawl
of body fur.

Long devout fingers
out of a blue Picasso.

This wolf's happiest
loping city blocks

where day after day
no face comes up twice.

He did his stint
in the swamp, and one

on the desert edge
of nowhere. His tail

dragged dust thick
as fuel exhaust

the whole way home.
Now, on a high bank

above the Hudson
he watches the barges,

ships being towed,
ice floes, the way

the bridge's lights
extend like comets

and shiver diving in.
When it's unusually still,

the lights remain
small round points,

a line of ellipses
trailing off …

Inside, his eyes warm
what they touch.

Smoothing her spine
like the open spine

of a prayer book,
he readies for night.

Drumming for the Matryoshka

Five-year-old Isabelle's
brought her nested dolls,

a brightly shellacked, wooden,
stoic Russian woman

that with a little twist
unscrews at the waist

and once divided in half
reveals another self

cupped inside the first,
the same color of borscht.

Only the smallest one,
the one they radiate from,

cannot be twisted apart.
She must be the heart.

While Isabelle plays hide and seek,
her mother and I try to talk,

though it doesn't really work.
She wants to play "Joan of the Ark,"

and line us up by twos,
but there are only two of us

and we refuse. What's next?
Her patience is overtaxed.

We've talked enough for one day.
There are other things to do.

The dolls need to wake up.
She shakes the one in her lap,

the one that doesn't unscrew,
small as my big toe.

The rest are scattered around.
She waves a majestic hand,

indicating the homes
of the various *grandes dames*:

one lives inside a saucer;
one's perched atop the toaster;

one's curled up with the cat,
unscratched, but glistening wet.

"We *must* drum them awake!"
She's sizing up the wok

and clutching a wooden spoon.
We make a great big din,

rattling the china saucer.
Something falls off the toaster.

The cat's out the door.
"More! More! More!"

Isabelle's ecstatic.
Her mother looks at the clock

and begins picking up
with a very decisive step.

The Matryoshka are put back together,
one inside the other,

closed with a final twist
and hugged to Isabelle's breast.

We hug each other in turn
and then, like that, they're gone.

Bosque del Apache

Winter. Scratchy branches flame
upward, stiff as ratted hair.
Crows crown the leafless trees—
black buds that bloom in unison
only to fly. At dawn, the marsh
is crowded as a skating rink;
ducks land in squadrons, swim
in pairs. Geese honk to be let by.
Like them, we're stalled in traffic,
caught in a cavalcade circling
the one-way fifteen-mile tour loop,
binoculars in every lap.
We scout to see what we're missing,
and end by missing what we're seeing.
The sky's too busy and too vast.
Lavender-orange masses of clouds,
lit from below, stagily surge
and disperse, while from the farthest East
daylight's dark stars flap their wings,
assume their shifting constellations,
and stream over us, crossing the sky
like corps de ballet after corps de ballet,
undulant velvet ribbons trailing.
Each bird, a basted stitch puckering
the sky's pale blue satin smock;
each flock, an intricate design
in thread the seamstress forgot to lick

and double-knot. And so it goes.
A *V* of cranes unravels, rivaling
the geese for noise.

Winged Victory

The motel, with its "pay per view,"
is more scenic than the scenic drive
and more exotic, with you
putting your forehead to mine
to check for fever, prescribing cola,
and charting our road, first with one finger,
then your whole hand ...

The next day it's tempting to touch
the cavern walls, but we don't,
knowing the oils we secrete
indelibly mar and stain.
Those draperies and columns, thrones
and soda straws—I'd like to see
the Winged Victory among *them*,

not to compare and choose,
but to be doubly bowled over.
The Winged Victory and what's left
of the Parthenon! But then,
when they turned out the lights
down there, seven hundred feet down,
and it was absolutely unlit,

pitch black, and for a moment
they had us hushed (until someone,
a crying child, broke the silence
and everyone began making noise),
wasn't that hair of a second in total

quiet and darkness, though fleeting,
one of the best moments yet?

That, and the amphitheater at dusk,
watching the cave's long exhalation
of bats, and then the first stars.
The world has so many ways to woo us,
so many unexpected vistas,
and miraculously so much of it (your face
at rest, eyeglasses off) near at hand.

In My Father's Eyes

The girl on the back page
of *WWD*,
in those days a trade
paper my father got
in the mail, was stepping off
the curb, wearing faded
boys' jeans torn at
the knee, huarache sandals
and a turquoise Mexican blouse.
Her picture was with others,
under the innocuous "Seen
on the Street" heading, not,
thank goodness, "in" or "out,"
but why the photographer knelt
down and aimed his camera
at her, the bulb flashing
as the traffic light turned green,
was, to my eye, obscure,
though as I looked and heard
my father say, "She looks
like you, ten years from now,"
I felt the heat of the flash
in my eyes as I shook my head,
laughed at him, and blushed.

The blouse was borrowed. It had
those oblong pointy buttons
carved like little spindles
that I used to think were made

out of ivory or bone,
but in fact are made of wood.
I was only in L.A.
to visit Kathy Fields,
my friend from summer camp,
the Montecito Sequoia
Summer Camp for girls.
It was she who lent me the blouse
to wear during my stay,
though no doubt had she known
it would catch the photographer's eye
she would have worn it herself,
for though we were together
crossing against the light
she wasn't in the picture.

My father didn't believe me
when I first admitted to him
that I was wrong to say
he'd been "out of his mind" to see
a family resemblance
between me and her, that she
was in fact my age, younger,
me, a few weeks, or months,
before. He looked again.
He didn't recognize
the shirt and wanted to know
where on earth it came from.
He fought to keep the pride
out of his voice and eyes
while he made sure of some things—

that my mother had known where I'd been,
that I'd not done anything wrong,
that I was, in fact, still his,
still interminably young.

Caffe Mediterraneum

Poseidon's ochre imperial eye
blandly surveys the café chairs
and pedestaled tables of his dominion,
watching unblinking over students
and all-day regulars who ply
their conversation like a trade,
nailing down each roughly held opinion
with a cigarette's emphatic tap-
tap-tap on the marble table top.
With perfect blind impartiality,
he stares at Julia Vinograd and me.
"You can look at it first, if you want,"
she says, hawking her new book
I looked at yesterday. Her braid
swings side to side and her leg brace
weighs her down as she walks away,
toward a tall thin girl with purple hair
who buys it at a glance.
May we all obtain such grace!
Poseidon oversees the fair exchange
but then must overlook two boys
who deftly slide flat palms across
napkin-and-saucer-littered tables,
pocketing the bus boy's change.

Poseidon's other eye is milky
from the smoke, its blue pupil
turned inward and oblivious.
Maybe he's thinking back to Greece,

or silently reciting Rilke,
but it's obvious that at least half
of his divided thoughts are far
from here. His empire, after all,
extends beyond the paneled wall
and smoky air of this café.
Time is his ocean, and the ocean's
his atmosphere. An ecru star-
fish and a conch shell spiral off,
float down to settle on his right,
evoking his kingdom with bubbles of ease.
Silver's assayed in the porous cupel
of his eye, while in my empty cup
the dregs and dross of yet another
afternoon spent drinking coffee
at the Med suggest to me my quotient
of such aimless days may be used up.
But who's to say? It's ten years
since I first looked into those dichot-
omous eyes, and they still hold sway.

This Rain

for MaLin

In Houston for the Agnes Martin show,
driving through its industrial barrio,
on our way to the port to see the postmodern urban
things you love: tin siding the color of bourbon,
barbed wire, big naval ships, enormous cranes
(not birds, but hoists), as I was changing lanes,
remember how I got a little lost?
You checked the map, and found the street we'd crossed
when I should have turned. We were both impressed how calm
and cool-headed we were, compared to *some*
we've driven with before, like the husbands we left
behind. We were cool, composed, collected as delft,
though I was glad we hadn't a tire to heft,
just the simple matter of turning back.
That's when we saw the corner storefront shack
of a church, stuccoed blue, plastered with placards,
the stenciled slogans custom-made for laggards
like us: "DO YOU KNOW WHERE YOU ARE HEADED?!" "TURN
OR BURN!!" As you said, nothing you couldn't learn
from Jenny Holzer or a sunblock ad.
I drove us by as slowly as I could,
but was too self-conscious to stop and make you wait
while I copied them down. Did you see me hesitate?
It was then, with a twinge, I missed Martin the worst,
an elemental feeling, like hunger or thirst,
I could repress for hours but not deny.
Often, like then, I missed him on the sly.
At dinner, their foibles made a rich foie gras;

we cracked their problems like a lobster claw;
but over coffee, muscat, and chocolate mousse,
we both turned tender, if a bit morose.
These days, what with disease, divorce, our lark's
lit up for me with innocent spritely sparks,
not unlike some paintings in the show—
the hand-drawn grids filled in with modest brio;
the monochromatic palette, soft on the eye;
gray-blues, more redolent of ocean than sky.
There's an inexplicable abstract human musk
the repeating lines give off—like rain at dusk—
an infinite sadness with an infinite joy—
love's twins, untwined only to be destroyed.

The Butterfly

The eye follows the hand,
the mind follows the eye,
the heart follows the mind.

—from the *Natya Shastra*

With no appreciable weight,
a butterfly alit

and rode my finger
an hour or longer.

Holding my hand ahead,
I let the butterfly lead.

We walked down to the kill,
its wings an upright sail.

I was almost afraid to breathe,
but my feet knew the path:

its trippy roots, the snagging branches
with springs like rocket launches.

I sat down on a rock.
I couldn't believe my luck.

The world right then seemed kind,
with a butterfly on my hand,

its bronze wings spread flat,
pulsing to raise its body heat.

Like a fluttering eyelash,
it tickled the web of flesh

between forefinger and thumb.
"My life can never be the same!"

I thought, studying the leopard spots
of its eyes; its veins like pleats;

its scalloped scales; its legs,
six knobby little twigs;

the thorax's fuzzy patina;
the two slender antennae,

bulb-tipped, like matchsticks;
and the pointed black circumflex

markings on each scored wing:
accents from the mother tongue.

Its proboscis sipped
the salt from my hand and tapped

out a secret code,
the secret names of God,

invisible to man,
imprinted on my skin.

If I could have become a fern—
a stone—a stalk of corn ...

Instead, my left hand twitched
and the butterfly detached

itself, all in a breath,
my article of faith,

momentarily tame
as if out of a dream,

now circling the rock,
not coming back.

Apple Blossoms

To follow the arc of the Big Dipper
as it leads to Arcturus, first I follow the arc

of your arm. In the sand at our feet, the stinkbug's
curved track, each step pronged and linked like vertebrae.

A snake spine could have left the same imprint,
but not a living snake. Rolling down the dune,

we spun together in one cocoon; at bottom,
splayed open, I surrendered to where I fell,

like a cart of apple blossoms overturned at the foot
of your bed. You say to use anything, *anything*.

Like the angels children flapping their skeletal wings
stamp in snow, the angels we made in the sand.

North Thailand Trek

Watery mud the color of rust
pooled in the lily pads of elephant tracks.
Army-issue green canvas rucksacks.
The tom-tom of wanderlust,

its smudgemarks all over the glossy 4x5s,
though now its echo's as inaudible
as the elephant's clanking wooden bell,
the crash of felled bamboo. Kitchen knives

stashed and sheathed in roof thatching;
under the floorboards, snuffling toward us,
a full-teated sow, slow as a tortoise.
Asleep, I thought her scratching

was at my side. My passport hung
like a Hand of Fatima around my neck.
Never so myopic as on that trek,
savoring the soporific smoke that clung

to my hair. In my hostess's red sarong,
hooped belt, and tassled sateen vest,
all urged on me by her children as I dressed,
I could make-believe I was Poolong,

one of the five hundred (so far)
who escaped the roving government troops
that took each harvest a third of the crops.
It was a nine-day walk from Myanmar—

a collective trauma, like a vein of ore,
that time's alchemical goldsmith
already's mining for a post-modern myth.
Told and retold, exile converts into lore

ancestral as the goddesses they say
men once lassoed and weighted with hoops,
their wings vestigial in our tassled tops,
their flights in dreams. The next day,

smoke-sick, toward a well-scrubbed
German-speaking girl in the crowded canoe
squinching her nose at the filthy Jew,
I fanned my reeking feet and grubbed

some extra space. For six hours,
knit like ribs across the hull,
we let the river gag and lull us, lull
and gag. What was sweet, sours.

In one double-exposed roll
of film, Buddha meditates mid-field.
The mind is a minefield,
pitted by the swirls on Buddha's soles.

The Jewish Cemetery at Penang

> And these sepulchral stones, so old and brown,
> that pave with level flags their burial place,
> seem like the tablets of the law, thrown down,
> and broken by Moses at the mountain's base.
> "The Jewish Cemetery at Newport"
> —*Longfellow*

In a patch of flattened weeds in front of the graves
where a Kohane's stone-carved fingers part to bless
the remains of Penang's departed congregation,
barefoot Malaysian boys were playing badminton,
a sagging string strung pole to pole their net.
Our Chinese trishaw driver, too old to read
the map without his glasses, with five hairs long
as my five fingers growing from a mole,
waited for us. He'd found the street although
the tourist map was wrong: the name no longer
Yahudi Road, but Zaimal Abidin.

A rusted lock hung open on a chain
slung loosely round the stone and iron gate.
From a tin-roofed shanty, a makeshift squat
just inside the walls, a woman watched us
unbuckle the chain and let it hang, the gate
creaking open enough for us to pass.

We walked past the boys, into headstone-high grass.
Lizards scuttled loudly to get away.
It looked decades since they'd been disturbed,
the newest markers twenty-odd years old;
no plastic wreaths; the only pebbles rubble

from the path, unpicked, unpolished, unplaced.
Dozens of graves, from the eighteen-thirties on.
Wolf Horn, Aboody Nahoom, Flora Barooth,
Semali Lazarus, Jacob Ephraim—
who but us had read these names this year?
Who alive could tell me who they were?

Pedaling us away, our spindly driver
had breath to spare, shouting against the traffic
what he'd found out while we were shooting roll
after roll of the cylindrical stone mounds:
there'd been a temple once, the Malaysian woman
had said, but nothing, no cornerstone, was left
of it, nor any living Georgetown Jews.
He himself was fifth-generation Malay,
and had no ties to China.

       Later, walking
along the arcaded five-foot ways, stopping
every few steps to gawk—at rows of shutters,
peeling plaster the color of robins' eggs,
cats with open sores, an Indian man
reading a Chinese woman's palm—you point
across the street to a small neighborhood mosque,
its minaret's crescent moon spiked
with crows. They scatter at the muezzin's call,
regather on a red-tile temple roof,
where Kuan Yin in her mercy guards her flock
and the air inside is smoky from our prayers.
A can of joss sticks rattles in my hand.
I fan the smoke toward her. What's one less temple

in a city of temples, a city of worship and trade?
What's one less altar? Over on Queen Street, when
the lime rind flares, lit with an oiled wick,
I place it in front of a jet-black Hindu goddess
whose bosom heaves for me as I make my rounds.

Sitting here, in a courtyard of our hotel,
on a stone stool, at a stone table, writing
the day's impressions down, I miss my God,
his featureless face imposing itself
among the more expressive others,
whom he himself has banished, but whom
I also love. Remember the beggar this morning,
in front of the Krishna Café, where we ate
using only our right hands, how he grabbed
your wrist in thanks, kissed the back of your hand
and wouldn't let go until I began to tug
at you from the other side? I saw the look
that swept your face and also—
he might have picked your pocket.

Last night, drinking at the E & O, I said
I'd spend all our money on one perfect
ruby, if only I knew where to find it,
how to recognize it, and its true worth.
After I scraped my knee in the monsoon gutter,
I thought of those cats, the open sores on their sides.
One bruise starts before the last one's healed.
To calm myself, I lit a stick of incense,
but now, though far from home, and despite myself,
I find I'm reciting what I know of the Sh'ma.

III
Another Part of the Field

for Katharine Weiser

Note

Each six-line poem was inspired by one of the hexagrams of the *I Ching*, the Chinese *Book of Changes*. There are sixty-four hexagrams in the *I Ching*; all but one of them are represented in these poems. Some of the hexagrams are returned to many times. The form of the stanza derives from the six lines with which a hexagram is constructed, and from the three coins (predominantly three beats per line) with which diviners "cast" those lines.

⁛

The wood, stacked high, kept dry
under the *portal*. A lit
fire, the smoke drawn straight up,
white doves fluttering above
my roof. Water steams
in the kettle, fragrant with herbs.

⁚⁚

Steam rises from the bronze vessel
filled with rice and broth.
On my knees I carry it
to the altar of my ancestors.
If the liquid doesn't slop,
if I pray, they are pleased.

⁛

I count my breath backwards
and forwards; I lift my spine.
At the crown of my head a nest
wobbles. The silver eggs
race round and round the rim
until I lift them out.

⁛

The earth, dry and sunken.
Up high, wind blowing through leaves.
Heaven seems just a dream,
farther away than ever.
If only for a cloudburst!—
to splash hands, face, feet, heart.

■

I wait, and nothing comes.
I wait, the light dies down,
the sun returns, the sun
shifts in the sky, the days
grow colder, warmer, cold
again. I practice. Wait.

■

My spine, a straight trail up
the mountain. I travel it
one vertebra at a time.
My thoughts stay close to home
and I keep them to myself,
that my sore heart may quiet.

■

Connected by a hoof-worn trail,
mountains stand back to back,
imposing bulwarks of strength.
I take the first to be
the highest, but the next
and next loom higher still.

■

One day, from the ridge top,
scanning Los Alamos,
the Jemez, billboards, our house,
I myself felt spied on,
and turned in time to meet
a coyote's intenser gaze.

###

Last night the last of the leaves
came flying down, wan flags
of surrender, drained and battered.
This morning, the trees are bare,
bereft, like monuments stripped
of gold, like cities plundered.

###

The bough shakes in the wind.
Dry leaves rattle down.
Soon the branch is bare,
shocking naked beauty.
When the wind comes up again,
will it also strip my heart?

###

Wind crinkles up the water
like a rippling cloth.
Gently stirred, miso
dissolves in the simmering broth.
I let go of something
I don't name—it's gone.

###

This morning we woke to rain.
Scratchy and faint, a dream
came over me in waves—
a late-breaking bulletin—
my sleep's last transmission
before signing off for the day.

※

Is it from modesty
that the sun descends and sets,
and modesty that makes
the full moon wane so soon?
As if in nature nothing's
upstage all the time.

※

"We like to think you got
the best of both of us,"
he'd say, then pause,
self-congratulatory, sly,
the punch line lying in wait:
"but your faults are all your own."

※

I am the youngest daughter,
the joyous lake, all mouth
and tongue, salty soil—
apparent gentleness,
that you who know me know
yields obdurate strength.

※

"Don't hide under a bushel!"—
a distant relative snapped,
going through the sales rack,
a vinyl miniskirt
and red angora sweater
held out for me to try.

■

A man showed up to clean
the pool and I was in it—
fifteen, naked, afraid
to stay in, afraid to get out,
until my mother came running,
livid, armed with a towel.

■

In this family model—
the love of son for father,
chasteness between husband and wife,
and loyalty of brothers—
where is the taut silken tug
of war between mother and daughter?

■

Bred thousands of years for silk,
the Chinese bombyx moth
is blind and flightless, but
the filament from its
cocoon is round, and stronger
than any other moth's.

■

Around the maypole, girls
lift their ribbons and run,
the silk streamers flying,
light with the colors of spring
and the inviolate buoyancy
of giddily prancing girls.

⁙

Pointing every which way,
the static compass rose,
composed of thirty-two
scrolled and petaled points,
leads nowhere, but divides
the conquered world again.

⁙

I hold the idea in hand
like a rough rock in my mind,
turning it over and over
until I forget it's there,
until one angle spasms
with light and I begin.

⁙

Ambition spooked me when
it bit, nibbling my ear.
I fingered the dormant mark
at night, daring it
to grow, then pushing down
on it, just in case.

⁙

I keep my eye on the line.
I never lift my head.
Conscientious and modest,
I review his oeuvre again,
but with each word I write
I make his poems mine.

###

Metaphor's sweet taste
on tongues that toy with it;
a root beer life saver's
brittle boiled sugar:
I suck till what was hard
dissolves, is absorbed.

###

My pile of books teeters,
my notes spill out of my arms
onto the table, like a lake
flooding the trees. I must
begin at once before
all thought's awash in debris.

###

Each day I write one verse,
like placing a stone atop
or beside another stone,
hoping a shape emerges,
a mandala, a maze,
a room, a house, a town.

###

I'm tired of waiting, tired
of how the days go by
planned in advance, set out
in a row like mailboxes.
It's tempting to smash them up,
catapult into his arms!

■

Rising above the earth,
the lake overflows the shore.
Our picnic, our clothes, drenched.
I stand with my wet hair,
apart, while others bustle—
unprepared, no candle, no prayer.

■

I look into a ravine
too deep too swift to cross;
I swallow my tongue instead
of spitting out the truth.
I'm weary of wariness,
but not ready to call a truce.

■

It's strange to look inside
and find one's heart a crater,
a moonscape steaming hot
and cold at the same time,
trampled and scarred by what
meteors, whose feet?

■

Where once I turned aside
and once you turned your back
and once we turned our lives
upside down and shook
the old solutions up—
now a corner's turned.

▦

We sit apart and look
into each other's eyes;
we coordinate our breaths,
blowing out in unison—
it always makes me laugh,
and I'm lifted on that wind.

▦

Too soon to tell and yet
each day I add a day
to my count I feel more sure:
until I'm gripped with fear
of the "what if"—what if
I go too far, am wrong?

▦

So many years we've been
each other's only love,
and now our daily prayer—
a candle burned all night
lit by this desire—
to share our lives with you.

▦

A germ of life inside
an almost hollow egg;
a lake stirred by the wind.
Brooding upon the waters.
The glint of a fishhook.
A line's shimmering cast.

⠿

These days of waiting: faith
is not the point, and hope
only makes minutes lag
like years: even my dreams
look the other way,
so I pretend as well.

⠿

The wind, rounding up clouds,
massing them into a herd,
like skittish thick-wooled sheep,
cannot itself make rain.
But everything is in place,
O love, for the cloudburst.

⠿

The nine-month revolution
seems to have begun:
a painless bloodless coup.
Only this to commemorate
the agonized years of doubt
preceding the new regime.

⠿

Sun sparkling on mica;
a stadium's standing ovation;
finger-in-mouth whistles
a boy learns to call his dog—
who comes, in leaps and bounds,
tail propulsively wagging.

▦

Cramps subsided and tears
dry. How long can one mourn
what never was? For a week,
light-hearted, I let my dreams
run free. A taste of that,
worth all this little pain.

▦

A wind that doesn't stop.
A rain that doesn't come.
Last night, my knees curled up,
our backs both turned away.
Silence like a siren.
The clock's monumental click.

▦

I'd be afraid to plunge
into the icy depths
of that raging ravine, my heart,
but I have no choice—it beats,
it surges on and on,
with or without my consent.

▦

Today it is a reserve
of love that keeps us tactful
and apart: our choice,
affection reaffirms
most days, but today our vows
in silence best are kept.

▦

Heaven rises, the earth
sinks, no current runs
between them, no harmony,
no trills of grace as birds
no longer flute the branches
of these gnarled and stunted trees.

▦

In its own time, the rain
will come, the seed will sprout.
Homilies of faith—
and the years pass. What else
is there to say or do?
Daubed with tears, with blood.

▦

Glum with winter, glum
as a student who didn't study
and failed all the exams,
in line for the bus home,
holes in his gloves, his socks;
his book of matches soaked.

▦

December: the sun sets
early now; the water's
frozen in our dog's pail.
Each morning we crack the ice
with a horseshoe, fling it out.
Some days it doesn't thaw.

■

I try to find my way
inside a cave in the dark.
I know an opening
exists. I feel my way,
using my hands, following
the contour of the cave.

■

Crossing the frozen river,
the fox is careful to keep
even the white brush tip
of his tail above the ice—
for once he got it wet,
and nothing would avail.

■

The calendar year clicks shut
tonight. The New Year's uncorked.
How will the first sip taste?
Hopes bubble up as we pour,
giddy already. Clink.
Clink. We hazard a toast.

■

Everything under the sun
illuminated and
revealed for what it is—
under the melting ice,
a rusted shot-out tub,
and then, underfoot, this joy.

⋮

What's held in two cupped hands—
and then the air we breathe—
the ground under my feet—
the lips I kiss and kiss—
a flame inside my heart
that flares and glows and dips.

⋮

Today I rearranged
my drawers and cabinets—
I stored my winter clothes
and stashed old manuscripts.
The garden, the fields, and I—
readying for spring.

⋮

After twenty years,
our last talk barely cordial,
over lunch you hand me
a carefully preserved
and love-washed portrait of
myself at seventeen.

⋮

The clouds have gathered; winds
have blown them across the sky.
They collect like dust in a corner.
My mind, too, is clouded—
the gale force of what's past
freshly stinging my face.

###

Carried across the lake
in the wind from the shade where she stands
on one leg, to the sunlit shallows
where the fledgling crane splashes
his wings, bites at the reeds,
looks up at her call, and comes.

###

It was his *voice*, soft growl
and grit of tenderness,
hypnotic timbre; the way
he checked to see was I
still there, the way his words
like cairns marked out the path.

###

To light and air, to dusk,
to morning dew, the sprout
breaks up the clods of dirt,
shakes free of dark damp earth,
neither muscling nor sidling,
but somehow pushing through.

###

Spring, and the kitten wakes
at dawn, mewing at the door—
best to get it done with
and let him out so I
can sleep. Through half-shut eyes,
a glimpse of the white half-moon.

▦

I'm on a train, gazing
at a line of tracks, your tracks,
long since derailed from mine.
Just how would it have been
had we linked up? I wonder—
happy though I am.

▦

My belly's full. I ate
the portion set before me.
My skin's soft from the bath;
my muscles, stretched and supple.
Does this make me content?
My mirrored eyes shine.

▦

It is good to have somewhere
to go, and good to find
friends there, where one has lived
and left. Last night, the night
before, dizzy excitement.
But today, it is home I long for.

▦

In the glare of sleeplessness,
gray is sharp as yellow.
Adamantine sky, hard glass
I see refracted in
the river, but not the river
in that rejecting sky.

▦

In the midst of crossing
in the middle of the street,
walking, looking up past
the tops of midtown's high-rises,
I hear one car slide near
and I leap to the other side.

▦

I see them at airports,
bald-headed boys, younger
each year; triangle caps
tucked into their belt loops,
their combat boots oddly
quiet on ramps and stairs.

▦

The crab apple outside
our kitchen was just beginning
to blossom the day I left;
the pale buds opening
but not yet open. Today,
home, the grass flecked pink.

▦

The ditch is running: water
bubbles as it flows
across the cut embankment;
it gushes out of the old pipe,
flooding an upper field;
in the lower, sheep graze.

■

A gaggle of geese, flying
north, over the mountain;
one feather falls, and floats
to the tallest pine, lands
on a cone, which drops to my hand
in time for the temple dance.

■

The bulbs barely up,
our April snow is mud;
and the sun gaining strength,
determined—is it really
time already to chop
and stack next winter's wood?

■

This year's peonies
have buds. Last year, transplanted,
they barely unfurled their leaves.
Could the same be said of us?
Two years in our new home,
and just beginning to bloom.

■

Rows of white hyacinth
came up under the arbor—
unexpected—like when you dug
a trench in the front drive,
unearthing those pint-size plastic
dinosaurs and cowboys.

⠿

Taking a walk last week
on a path just off the road,
I saw a camisole,
lavender laced with black,
hanging from a piñon bush,
just four wheeler height.

⠿

At the entrance to the arroyo,
we walked around the lamb,
its rib cage open and empty,
wool lying on the ground
in drifts, like cottonwood snow,
coyote scat nearby.

⠿

We scrubbed graffiti off
and patched the mud-brick walls;
we killed some thirteen mice
in a week; we took both cats
and the dog for shots; you checked
the deed, I answered calls.

⠿

Negotiating a deal,
we counter our own offer
before we even make it;
we calculate a sum,
then split it into parts
to add it up again.

■

At the slumber party,
it comes out that four
out of seven of us color
our hair; five wear makeup.
One husband is disparaged—
the rest, in silence, go free.

■

Peace marches, happenings,
be-ins; the grass littered
with love; one large picnic,
everyone sharing their sandwiches—
at twelve I closed my eyes
to be among such friends.

■

I think of Anne Frank peeling
potatoes, listening
to others argue, and
writing it all down.
I think of *her* first kiss,
not mine, in the blackout dark.

■

We wore black leotards
and snake bracelets; at lunch
we smoked hashish on the lawn.
We knew the word *Rorschach*.
We analyzed the clouds,
xeroxed our feet and palms.

■

At boarding school her talk
was the first hard liquor I drank.
I liked the way it went
right to my head; I gulped
it down, gullible then,
and never yet hungover.

■

That summer I woke to want.
It never left me. Sex
and sleep appeased me only
to show me what it was
I wanted more of, more,
and none of it enough.

■

"Boasting's all talk, young girls
say anything they please
only to impress each other,"
my mother shook her head,
knowing I loved stories
indiscriminately as fruit.

■

The dream was an injury—
how languidly she stretched,
imperceptibly flexing her claws;
how little she needed to say.
And there was no puncture wound
when I woke—only an abscess.

⊞

Hair gleaming black, cat's sheen,
fingers coral-tipped and
tapered, sapphire-eyes
I wanted too much from,
and from that mouth, that said
"come share what I bestow."

⊞

I can't seem to reach down
far enough into myself
to reach the cool pure water
of words. Today the rope
is not long enough, or else
the bucket's sprung a leak.

⊞

We never had a well
in the suburbs of California,
at least not a well I saw.
Our water came from a tap,
from pipes, from paying the bill.
Money was our reservoir.

⊞

In yesterday's flash flood,
coming down the mountain,
the usual rivulets
we wade or hop across
breached their banks to form
one mud-brown churning braid.

■

I heard the loud blunt thunder,
saw the jagged crossed swords.
My neighbor's horse, struck dead,
lies in the arroyo still.
Too heavy to move. Ribs clean,
skin rough and worn, like burlap.

■

Amid the Fourth of July
sparklers and fireworks,
a naked man, bleeding
on his street, in his hands, a knife.
Against a garden wall,
police surround him and shoot.

■

Open-faced, huge-headed,
its coarse neck bent, the sun-
flower's made devout by weight.
From its bright face that nods
toward earth a micro-sun,
the seeds plash down like tears.

■

The pregnant mare stripped
our trees, chewing the bark
of all the Russian olives
like nicotine gum, and so
we had to move her off
the field before she foaled.

▦

Circling up the mountain
I think only of the lake
that rests on the mountaintop.
To swim with you in the sun-
heated clear blue water!—
and so my feet keep on.

▦

First mist, then wind, then rain.
The sun, steaming a hole
through loose watery clouds.
Rushing down the mountain,
wanting to get back for breakfast,
I run up against a rainbow—

▦

When heaven and earth first met
in a squall of thunder and rain,
the rainbow's silken threads
were knotted, tangled, weedy:
it took deft hands to plait
that otherworldly bridge.

▦

Carried over the threshold,
her eyes take time to adjust;
future and past drop off,
one spiked heel at a time.
He sets her, barefoot, down:
his arm the nearest rail.

▦

Trajected into space
on marriage's fixed elliptic,
entwined like twin stars,
pulsating light and heat,
sometimes to collide,
sometimes to dream and drift.

▦

On the day of our departure—
too early to read the meaning
of "opposition"—I'd like
to ignore the way the words
"having the vehicle dragged"
make my stomach churn.

▦

The first leg of the journey:
deceptively familiar,
as if our destination
were no farther than home:
driving down 280,
we count the shades of green.

▦

Fog is to clouds, like milk
to cream, or like whipped egg whites
before the peaks stand stiff,
the bowl turned upside down.
But fog dripping through pines
should not be mistaken for rain.

###

Another part of the field.
Another herd of cows.
Someone else's ax
to grind before I chop
and stack his cord of wood,
before his barn's my bed.

###

To safeguard that the land
be untouched by royal blood,
a deposed Thai king
was put in a velvet sack
before being bludgeoned to death
with fragrant sandalwood clubs.

###

"We could go in and cream
the side that's killing all
their neighbors—but what happens
when we leave? I've seen
an arms bazaar, the weapons
heaped up like fruit, like spice."

###

We'd better make some plan—
plane or overnight
express, or air-con bus,
and where to stay when we
arrive—we'd better map
it out, or else stay put.

▦

Today we saw the hills
of Burma and Laos across
the Mekong, through the mist:
the Golden Triangle.
Unable to cross the border,
we wet our hands and feet.

▦

Miles behind the lines,
far from the field of action,
the field of blood and death,
is another field, a field
of orange poppies, blue
flax, dreams, and rest.

▦

Through the window, rice fields
blur the miles while palm trees
stamp them, and Brahman cows,
girls in school skirts, houses
built on stilts, until
my passport's slid back full.

▦

Three days in the same place:
we seem almost settled—
breakfast at the Krishna,
drinks at the E & O,
hand wash drying on chair backs
while we read guidebooks and maps.

⊞

I hardly know myself!
Tonight I gladly traded
that friendly guest house for
a private bath and shower,
an air-con hotel room
with separate single beds.

⊞

Under a mosquito net
in an A-frame beach "chalet"
on the South China Sea,
memorizing Malaysian.
At *tenga hari*—noon—
the ferry will pick us up.

⊞

Tropical desert ocean.
The sun doubles going down.
Last night the moon was full
and was eclipsed. Your arms,
that encompass and contain.
The cascading bougainvillea.

⊞

Everybody laughing—
because what the old man says
is funny?—or because
we can't understand a word?
I'm sure he's describing the war,
and tell him I know he was brave.

▦
The ocean's lapping up
six coconuts that fell
to the lip of its bowl in the night;
of those three pineapples
we bought off the truck—enough
for one each day—one's left.

▦
"Can you see the body?"
He prodded me nearer the pyre
and I saw a charred foot fall
as a cigarette was lit
off a splinter of kindling
laughingly held in the flame.

▦
A mosquito whined in my ear;
a child cried once, and one
rooster crowed, setting off
his minions, thousands of dogs
who barked at the heels of my dreams
scurrying home before dawn.

▦
Cold showers the last two weeks.
Tomorrow I'm thirty-eight.
Last night's mosquito coil
filled my head with smoke.
Will the offerings on the ground
placate *both* demons and dogs?

⠿

The lap of luxury
indeed is softly padded—
is the gamelan by the pool
playing just for us?
By candle flame, a pearl's
blistered flaw's lustrous.

⠿

Back to the Puri Saaren,
Ubud's Palace Inn,
with birds in cages singing
from the courtyards' gilded eaves
and stone demon guards,
krises up their sleeves.

⠿

Corners looped and pinned,
seven veils hung out
to dry on the laundry line
undulate in the wind.
She leaves them up all day,
letting the mystery air.

⠿

As if between here and there,
Scylla and Charybdis,
in wait for my little skiff,
crouch in a narrow strait
like muggers in an alley,
I dread the long way home.

⁂

I feel like being ill-
behaved, and telling that
girl what I think of her
and her shenanigans.
Don't bother! he says to me,
her flame's already ash.

⁂

Merciless August highlights
the split in our bed's grain,
trying to heighten old
resentments left from that time
it was our battlefield.
The much-rubbed wound shines.

⁂

Whittled down to nothing,
the moon blacks out, goes spin-
ning off; comes to a day
or so later, sharp as a scythe.
Meanwhile, the stars swarm,
bees following their queen.

⁂

Were you the cat in the jaws
of the chow Renata found,
poor thing, one paw chomped off,
all rolled in mud, now buried?
Brave Puck, short life of scrapes,
once pillowed by my hair.

⁙

In what name shall we meet?
Whose footsteps shall we follow?
What ritual unfold?
The nations intermingle.
Earth shrinks under the lens.
Whose hands will gather us in?

⁙

Not cracked, my mind, but wobbly,
unsteady in my hands
as a broken-legged pot,
half its contents spilled
on the walk before I reach—
but I do—my own front door.

⁙

Though water itself, set loose,
is inexhaustible,
a lake holds only so much
before it overflows:
learn your own dimension
before saying no or yes.

⁙

Because we're early, we walk
an extra block, picking
flowers and gossiping.
Inside, our teacher smiles.
The letters are black flame.
My spirit spins like a dreidel.

⁜

Two handfuls of sod, the grass
still growing; Ganeshe, shipped
from overseas. Your voice,
the timbre of forged metal,
a date for our rendezvous,
ink still wet on the page.

⁜

Three long tables set
under the *sukhos* branches.
A blessing over the wine.
We wash our hands, recite
another prayer, and then
the blessing over bread.

⁜

And now the arroyo's dry wash,
the shifting ridge of hills,
are wave and ocean bed
to me. The juniper,
crenelated coral,
a shell, the shard in my hand.

⁜

The flute notes of grace,
the quiet candle flame,
water in a carafe,
the moon floating above
the mountain, birds at dusk,
a glimpsed afternoon star.

⠿
Yesterday at Shul,
I sat with the other women,
gauze filtering our sight
of the Ark, now open, now closed.
From the men's side arose
the cacophony of prayer.

⠿
No coins to toss, I chose
"obstruction": nemesis,
unbypassable
barrier to my will;
fallen roadside boulders
to pick my way through.

⠿
To sort through the self's forces,
to sift with a mining pan
desires, to see without
illusion, the eye cleansed,
breath deep, nose sniffing
the wind—to know the self ...

⠿
"You've misunderstood *retreat* "
a strategician friend
told me. "It's undertaken
in strength; it's not defeat."
And so these end: with one
of the sixty-four stones unturned.

1993-1995

The following index correlates the poems, by first line, to a hexagram of the *I Ching*. The numbering and titles of the hexagrams are taken from the Bollingen Baynes/Wilhelm translation.

COLOPHON

Set in **Dante**,
a face of elegant legibility
in the Renaissance tradition,
but designed by Giovanni Mardersteig
in mid-20th century appreciation—
it should continue beautifully
in the next millenium.

•

Book design by J. Bryan

Carol Moldaw was born in Oakland, California, in 1956 and grew up in the San Francisco Bay Area. She holds an A.B. with honors from Harvard College and a M.A. from Boston University. Magazines in which her poems have appeared include *The Kenyon Review*, *The New Republic*, *The New Yorker*, *Partisan Review*, *Threepenny Review*, and *Triquarterly*. A recipient of an NEA Literary Fellowship in 1994, Moldaw settled in New Mexico in 1990 and lives in Pojoaque, 20 miles north of Santa Fe. Her first book of poems, *Taken from the River* (Alef Books), was published in 1993.